THE DAYS I DREAM OF

Chocolate

Second Edition

3 5 7 9 10 8 6 4

Saint John's, Antigua
West Indies

First printed in July 2022

Images from Canva ©

Visit the author's website at
https://lmsanguinette.wordpress.com

DEDICATION

This book of poems is dedicated to my dearest friends, who have inspired me with their various stories of love and longing.

"In love's tenderness, I find the colours one cannot see and the sounds one cannot hear, yet I paint and sing with them regardless."
~L. M. Sanguinette

THE DAYS I DREAM OF

Chocolate

A COLLECTION OF POEMS

L. M. Sanguinette

CONTENTS

ACKNOWLEDGMENTS

Writing a poetry collection is a curious task. A poem on its own is a perfectly contained universe in a few lines. A collection requires more planning and thought, and especially cohesion. I have written poetry for years, but only recently have decided to bind my poems together, something that required the creation of something altogether different, more along the lines of a novel, and yet nothing like a novel at all.

If a poem is a flower, a collection is a manicured garden, with channeling pathways to guide the reader into deeper stretches of the imagination, whereby each step—each turn of the page—pulls them along on a journey they had not previously imagined. This is something I only realized after writing my first collection and working with my editor to create something engaging. So many things have changed since I started out on my writing journey, and I am forever grateful for all of the twists and turns and wild rides that it has put me through. The experience of writing deserves its own acknowledgment, as it is one of learning and growth, such themes which can be found in various poems in this very collection.

I'd like to thank the various people throughout my life that have inspired these poems, some of whom have been my greatest friends, others my greatest loves. One of my favourite quotes about love comes from the book *The Night Circus* by Erin Morgenstern, and many of these poems take inspiration from this quote.

"I have had affairs that lasted decades and others that lasted for hours. I have loved princesses and peasants. And I suppose they loved me, each in their way." ~ Tsukiko in The Night Circus by Erin Morgenstern

Regarding the persons involved in this endeavour, I'd like to thank my editor for working with me to make my dreams come true. I would never have had the courage to publish this series without her. She keeps me motivated even through the toughest of slumps and reminds me that my goals are closer than they seem.

I'd also like to thank my partner, who keeps me grounded and sane during these projects. He reminds me constantly that the only failure would be in not trying and pushes me to keep going when I feel I cannot carry on. He is the reason I keep many of the deadlines I do, and for that and more, I am forever grateful. Thank you for being my rock and helping me weather the various storms.

Finally, I'd like to thank my family, who have always supported me and my various—sometimes outlandish—choices in life. Some of them still have no idea that I have published but stand steadfastly behind my endeavours; others were surprised by the first collection and have unexpectedly become my biggest fans. My goal is to continue making you all proud.

INTRODUCTION

This book is the second in the **Days I Dream** series, the first title being ***The Days I Dream of Coffee***. This series is not only decorative but delightful in nature, intended initially as personal gifts to my friends and loved ones that I decided to share with the world.

This collection pertains specifically to the trials and tribulations of love, and all phases of such love: beginning, middle, and end. Chocolate was chosen as the motif, not only for my own love of the treat, but because it is so closely associated with the idea of love. So much so that I can no longer remember whether the idea for a collection of love poems came first or if the title did.

This collection is comprised of experiences in the form of poems, of which some are my own, some are representations of other love stories, and some are simply evocative but fictitious experiences. The idea of love and the experience of it are two things very personal in nature. My goal with this collection is to provide snippets of experiences that evoke scenes in the imagination of the reader.

This collection contains a variety of poem styles ranging from brief commentaries with defined rhyming schemes to larger tales, becoming more narrative in nature. The collection is broken into five different sections based on the type of love being referred to in the poems.

WHITE CHOCOLATE

A dreamy version of the treat hailed throughout the ages, white chocolate was first commercially produced in the 1930s and made from cocoa butter, sugar, milk, cream, and vanilla.

The following poems are as dulcet and dreamy as their chocolatey counterpart, made to reflect the aspirational and sometimes even fantasized version of love most often talked about in fairy tales and classic love stories. This kind of love is also found at the start of a relationship, where we wear our rose-coloured glasses and see only perfection.

Great for a quick pick-me-up that's short, sweet, and leaves a gentle longing in your heart.

LOVE BE MY TENDER

love be not my keeper but my tender
so that sunlight may shine brighter than gold
where the dewdrops cling to rosebush petals
with thorny trunks and tangled roots
and not to paper-wrapped bouquets

EYES LIKE YOURS

poems could be written
about eyes like yours
the way they consume me,
wholly, longingly, lovingly
as though nothing else matters
and how I could never pull mine away,
as a bird could never be held aground
and like the bird my own feet, too,
shall never again touch the floor.

FIRE TO TOUCH

the touch of your fingers
leaves ardent trails of flames
along the lines you blaze
down my cheeks—down my throat
—sends shivers through my spine
where passions will combust
in vibrant ecstasies,
and in silent stillness
blanketed by the night
the world around hitches
as our two bodies burn.

MARVEL AT YOUR DIVINE

i marvel at all the ways
the light touches your soul
the wind carries your heart
the sun reflects your fire

i cherish all the things
that make you special
that make us different
that make this divine

i treasure the nights
and days we spend
together and give thanks
that your love is mine

WISHING STARS

And like the babe I once again
find myself wishing on the distant suns,
hoping much like the explorers of old,
their light will guide me to a promised home.

Where passion lines the bedsheets
and honesty makes my tea,
and kindness sits beside me
in all her generosity.

Where patience cleans the kitchen
and forgiveness sweeps the floors,
and laughter dances between us
while loyalty latches the door.

And like the babe I know not how
or when it will come my way
but deep down in my heart of hearts
I know love will come to stay.

PAIN AU CHOCOLAT

I dream of all the trips we'll have
to London, Athens, Brussels, Cannes,
the stradas we'll walk in Napoli,
the ruas in Porto and Canterbury.

The days in Munich, Geneva, and Vienna
the operas, football, and wine cellars.
In Bucharest and Budapest, we take photos together
huddled tight in colder weather

I dream of Paris and the food we'll eat
I dream of Monaco and the people we'll meet
I dream of Rome and all her glory
I dream of Madrid and her tender story

of starlit nights on empty streets
of history's shadows lining our feet
of coffee dates in quainter parts
to share a *pain au chocolat*

THE EDGE OF THE SUNLIGHT

I find you
at the edge of the sunlight
where my vision wants to blur
—but doesn't
where my heart should beat steady
—but quivers
where the edges of my lips curl up
and I, with my mere mortal soul,
cannot restrain them

FAIRYTALES

fairytales have forced my mind
to imagine the worlds where
two hearts beat as one
and only one other
may fill the gaps
in my soul

THE WATER'S TOUCH

may I be held as the ocean a shell
coddled and swathed in the embrace of the sea
so not even light may pry its watery grasp
as it fills the gaps leaving no space between

HEAVEN'S FALLEN ANGEL

I'd never seen an angel
until you crossed my path,
shining under moonlight
bathed in mystery, swathed in black.

Heaven's clouds have lost an angel
to the firm and dirty ground
but not even the grime and grunge
could strip you of your glow.

A GLANCE IN YOUR DIRECTION

It's just a chance,
that glance in your direction,
but I think I spot a flame,
a glimmer from your chocolate eyes
that makes me wish to ask your name.

It's just a thought,
a split-second in time is all
but it brings that curl to your lips
the kind that stands the hair on my arms
and suddenly the room around feels warm.

It's just a look,
but it speaks more than words
a magnetic attraction that pulls at our feet
slowly but surely, we stroll the floor, weaving
through the crowd with more in mind than hello.

I SPY

burdened by much of fate's tangled twine
we walk the intersections of our lives
with all the buzzing of the world around
noises and distractions abound
yet no amount of humdrum or commotion
nor even our crossing trains' locomotion
pulled apart by the directions we drive
could take your eyes from mine.

DESIRE

it is desire which feeds my mind
and drives my will to move
whereby this desire
so guides my feet
on the path that
leads to you

FORTUNATE WOULD IT BE

fortunate would it be
to wake up to that
which in dreaming state
do i so desire
where in the night's
most pleasant sleep
compares not with a reality
that sees you laid down
peacefully at my side.

THE ROMANCE THAT COULD'VE BEEN

like two passing ships we glide
through tangles and fates intertwined
crossing arms over cautious chests
wondering what should be
—what could be
if society didn't bind us to
opposite ends of lingering space
where all the words we will ever say
are emotions warped by truth's heavy lies
that seem harder to speak
though free speech be the name of the game
yet here we sit
face to face and separated by
transparent walls held in place by titles
where you watch our trains pass by
ignorant or else uninterested
or possibly—if by that glimmer in your eye
like me dare not ripple what waves might make
anxiously contemplating all we are
and all that's hidden within
seated here enamoured of
the romance that could've been.

HOW LONG

How long have I been blind?
How much longer have you pined?
How long have you waited
with only me on your mind?
How long have you watched me
as I self-destructed?
How long have you longed to
be he whom I trusted?
How long have you needed
to see me at your side?
How long have you pleaded
with the tears that I cried?

—Long but not longer than you have been asking,
though still I am waiting for your true unmasking.
For you to admit it, that you feel it too,
and see me and love me
the way I do you.

METROMANCE

I catch a glimpse of your pensive eyes
as they flit back and forth from me to your screen
with a tentative smile curling at lustful lips
wondering what this all could mean.

You too spy with your hazel eyes
a look of longing and interest growing
in the bite of my lip and the scrunch of my brow
things you wish for without showing.

I smile and you smile back
in an act that is apprehensively earnest
from opposite sides of the crowded metro car
though from vision fade all the rest.

You think it not polite to ask
the name I wear that you long to speak
guessing at all that might fit my body
in case chance would have us cordially meet.

And conversations maintained
between stolen glances and invisible overtures
accompany us on our brief romance
until our sudden departures.

THE FIRST DATE

unsteady and unprepared i wait
patient on air with a stomach in knots
feet rocking back and forth
on the pavement that won't keep still.

the headlights roll up in the dim of the night
beckoning me forward, into the unknown
part of me wonders if my bed will miss me
but my face is made up, even if my mind is not.

and your smile shines in the light of the stereo
while i thank the dark, for it hides my blush
as we drive off deeper into the night
me wondering what revels you have in store.

the cinema screen lights up and plays
and in its glow your eyes meet mine
i catch you spying at the way
the film highlights the dimples in my smile.

i lean so my hair may curtain my face
the way velvet would've the screen but decades prior
shying away from the gaze you give me
that should belong to the screen but hasn't for a time.

you lean in for the kiss i already expect
and after i'll rest my sleepy head on your chest
and we'll forget for a stint that we aren't alone
as the credits roll but i know we have only just begun.

BLOOMING

And so I bloom
under your gaze
growing red as the roses
that line the garden trails,
these paths I once walked alone
and admired a different way.

And so I bloom
petal over petal
revealing my many depths
bearing the soul that should
only be mine, but to which
I have offered you the key.

And so I bloom
despite the falling night
when all the flowers curl again
recoiling in for another day's rest
I unfurl, blooming brighter than them all.

MILK CHOCOLATE

The classic treat is derived from cacao and cacao butter, and made through a process of fermenting, roasting and grinding cacao beans until they become a smooth paste, and then tempered until it reaches the optimum texture for what we know as chocolate.

The following poems tackle the emotions behind being in love. This stage of love is not all rainbows and sunshine; rather, it is when two people begin to strip themselves down bare and reveal their true colours, for better or worse, until there are no falsehoods between them.

These poems are the perfect balance of sweet and bitter, and just like the classic chocolate recipe, are great for any time of day.

LOVE'S HEART

may all hearts be as calm as
the one that walks
into the uncertainty
of true love
and beats
in steadfast
tranquility

LOVE AS SWEET AS CHOCOLATE

Love as sweet as chocolate
embraced by warmth divine
to colour red my frozen cheeks
and darker secrets passions keep
through kisses under trellised vines.

DIRTY DISHES

you will wash my dirty dishes
while i clean your room
faceless and without recognition
these tasks that keep us together
but threaten to rip us apart

they show face in every argument
when our voices rise above
the sounds of our pleading hearts
as they still beat for one another
yet we are too dumbed to hear

howling monkeys we become
over things that mean nothing
but hurt like nothing before
'til i cry waterfalls and you swear buckets
until we find the intersection

where you'll wash my dirty dishes
and i'll still clean your room
so each morning i can have a clean bowl
and each night you a clean bed
and together we can start anew.

TO SPEAK THOSE WORDS

Sometimes when I say I love you
I mean I need you to stay
To hold together my broken bits
and keep the pain away

Sometimes when I say I love you
I mean you're being an ass
And you've done something—once again
to make me want to laugh

Other times when I say I love you
I mean to say please don't go
I'm scared of the world without you near
and wish not to be alone

But there will be one 'I love you'
that is said with nothing behind
the day I choose to bare my soul
all splintered parts of the broken whole
shedding the pride to which I hold
leaving the honest and unrefined.

IN YOUR WAKE

My love will go
to he who walks
among the trees
and naked vines
whose tread leaves
none but flowers.

UNDER THE SUN'S GLOW

nothing compares to the gentle glow
of rays whose light filters through
the facades and charades of reality
to seek peace in the brown of your eyes.

HOW MY MIND WANDERS

I see you
in the smile of a passing child
the way your cheeks light at the sight of me.

I hear you
in the songs that float on the wind
the melodious symphony of your infectious laugh.

I feel you
in every blanket's warm embrace
paling in comparison to the radiance of your heart.

My mind often wanders, in stray moments of bliss
to the sound of your chest
the feel of your lips

the sight of your smile
your breath
touch.

Over a simple cup of coffee, bitter and true
I like how my mind always wanders
to you.

FIRST LOVE

Let's be lovers like the ones we see on T.V.
let's dance around ballrooms and play in the snow
let's get caught up in moments, forget how to breathe
let's watch all the sunsets and steal kisses by the sea.

Let's lay awake at night afraid to close our eyes
for fear that no dream could ever be so sweet,
let's buy a great house on a beach somewhere
and start the family we'll treat better than ours did us.

Let's stay in all day and watch movies in bed
under rainy skies and blankets warm
as we sip on hot chocolate (leave cream on our noses)
and ignore Time, who wishes to move on without us.

Let's be first loves, but good loves
the kind that never fades or falters,
let's argue but make better the bond we share
and begin new days with ever stronger minds.

Let our hearts be true and our egos not shallow
and let the world call us crazy…

They will call us crazy…

Crazy for it is this world we know,
the same world that could never describe us…

This us, this love…

This first love, this true love
this pact and promised love…

Our love.

LOVER'S PLAIN

Many a cloud rolls over the horizon
readying for a storm to us still unknown
with lust and longing to yet consume
as the hearts we hold be not our own.

Fallen fast and fallen slight
enamoured of the waiting rain
whose promise of greener lands will keep
bountiful harvests on lover's plain.

THE LITTLE THINGS

The little things a heart desires
attention and trust passion inspires
where holding hands are pacts unspoken
and forehead kisses are locks unbroken
where truth speaks through transparent glass
and scars are only marks of the past
trivial and inconsequential to a new love's care
under which darkened traumas disappear
these little things mark good from great
and offer praise to a lover's fate.

A BOX OF CHOCOLATES

I fell for you the day you placed
the box of chocolates on my desk
not out of some prosaic persuasion
or misguided romantic jest.

I fell for you with each sweet bite
of every chocolate's flavoured surprise
the way you watched the way I thought
with longing in your eyes.

I fell for you—and all sides of you
like the bonbons you had brought
after hearing me say how I loved the treat
a comment you'd not forgot.

HOT SOUP IN BED

Here you come with a bowl of hot soup
ushering me into our bed
with snot dripping down my nose
and socks covering my freezing toes
you put your hand on my boiling head.

You know that I am overworked
and burnt out like the candlewick
that we have yet to toss because
we've been busy running up and down
from stress—no rest—to sick.

But you bring me hot soup in bed
and wrap me up in blankets tight,
force medicine down my swollen throat,
lay next to me and hold me close
so I can sleep through the night.

A NIGHTTIME DRIVE

We fell for each other under starlit skies
and forgot in the fog of the quotidian blues
the bliss we once got on our nighttime drives
but tonight is a break in the haze.
Sifting papers and shuffling feet
replaced by sunset pictures and stereo high
listening to songs our parents heard new
that we've borrowed or stolen for our own hint of joy
to fill the silence we'd let grow between us
but tonight silence has taken his leave.
In the din of the night, nothing looks brighter
than the gleam of your smile
and the glow of your eyes
that remind me of the you I once knew
who carried me out for a nighttime drive
away from prying eyes
so that we two may fall in love.

LOOK AT THE GRANDS

Look at the grands dear, playing in the mud,
I think with a little laugh that rattles my lungs.
Many years back those two were us
chasing childhood's many ghosts
and picking at things we shouldn't touch—but did.

Look at the grands dear, clomping about in the rain,
as we watch from the porch of the house
we built long before they were born
but was clearly built for them.
The garden was made to make them smile,
the fence to keep them safe and sound,
the trees I planted only for fruit
were made for our monkeys to climb.

Look at the grands dear, you say and I smile.

Our grands, I nod, for you've been watching,
I know that it hurts you and cures you as it does me,
to see all we've made not go to waste
under our older hands as the young ones play.

Our grands… you sigh and I do too,
for we know that Time is calling us soon
but has given us grace and space to enjoy
the tail end of life reflected in their little faces.
And part of me wonders if I don't see
the ghost of my own grand smiling back in the mirror
watching a lifetime away.

WHEN THE WORLD GOES DARK

You promise me the world,
you promise me your heart
but will you still be at my side
when the world goes dark?

—The world goes dark each night, my dear
when the sun hides its face,
though the moon takes charge of us
I'm still here in my place.

But will you stand beside me when
our prides make love seem hard?
Will you still be here with me
when I show my scars?

—I will stand beside you when
your scars tell you to fight
I'll be here to wipe your tears
and hold you through the night.

But will you then grow weary when
my terrors make me numb?
Will you toil here at my side
when I'm no longer fun?

—Never has it crossed my mind
that you are not the one
whether we dance or do nothing at all
we will always be fun.

—I promised you the world, my love
I promised you my heart,
I'll still be here when the skies aren't clear
and when the world goes dark.

DARK CHOCOLATE

This no-fuss, no-frills version of the classic treat is the base of each bar. This type of chocolate is raw, bitter, and filled with undertones that can only be noted when the initial longing for sugar is over. To some, this true treat is insufferable, yet to others, it is a delicacy beyond compare.

The following poems are also no-fuss and no-frills, and though they may seem bitter at first, their purity shines through, raw and tasteful in the end. These poems touch on the darker sides of romance, such as unrequited love, heartbreak, and betrayal.

These poems, like their chocolatey counterpart, can only truly be enjoyed with experience.

WINTER SHOWERS

the winter showers
and their particular powers
refresh the bougainvillea's flowers
and the coconut palms that look like towers

a heartbroken girl sits beneath
having adamantly refused to eat
watching the grey clouds roll in in sheets
wondering who too made them cry

PINING

pining over people
who won't spend time with me
not even a couple of hours
not even a cup of tea

pining over people
whose hearts don't skip a beat
whose smiles are given in earnest
but whose eyes with mine don't meet

pining over people
whose lips mine will not part
not even will they speak the words
I long for in my heart

so I pine over people
who'd never pine over me
who'd never share a blushing stare
or even a cup of tea

LOVER'S SCORN

we will meet again
when all the seeds i planted
in your barren ice become
roses with no thorns

SCORCHED

Scorched be the heart
that feels only regret
for all that was done
and in remembrance
sheds not a tear

MIND OF STORMS

figments of fictitious fervor
make fragments of a fractured mind,
when widows weather weary storms
by cowering as quiet's concubine.

and battered, bruised, and bitter sleep
make better the demon's broken bed,
forged in fire's forgotten freedom
keeps tethered and taught the widow's head.

MEMORIES OF WAR

There are little things scattered
about the lanes of life I have walked,
which my mind clings to in adamance
like barnacles on ship hulls
and fire to dried brush.

The memories of harder times
when I was *more* and made to feel *less*
broken, for I couldn't be molded
where jagged edges were filed down
doubt made cracks to weaken my structure.

My heart still beats uneven and unsteady
as the memories of war creep slowly back in
passing places I thought I'd never more see
nor feel whole standing within
and still I know I can breathe.

The stranger days of mindful violence
have long since passed, and I may wonder
what all the shattered panes of doubt still do
in the foundations I have built upon and if
they wait to be made into windows again.

But I have weathered darker storms than these
the fictitious fighting my mind has made
but my heart repels in any case,
reminding me of where I began and how far
I have come to stand again.

THE DEMONS I FALL ASLEEP WITH

You are not enough, they say
this inner choir of wicked demons
that I let make my bed
not pretty, not smart, not wanted, not loved
it doesn't matter what you do,
or which soul you show your aching heart to,
you'll never be good enough.

You're not the Cinderella
that will ever get her prince,
you'll have no happy endings,
or hopeful new year's kiss
you my dear, and listen clear, will never ever be
despite what longing makes you think
good enough for any of this.

You cry way too much,
you never learned to trust
you'll never nearly be worthy, they say
of anyone's truest and honest love
so cast aside longing and frivolous lust
it's time, my dear, for you to give up
your pathetic attempt to be anything but.

Now rest your eyes and steady your head
we'll fluff your pillows and make your bed
we the demons your worries keep
your nightmares tether to eager feet
and keep you safe from love's broken bust
for who can you trust more than us
to watch over you as you fall asleep.

THE TIMING WASN'T RIGHT

When we met the stars collided
when we met the world felt right
in your arms the pain subsided
leaving only love's tender bite.

When you held me my oceans stilled
in your gaze my heart took flight
like an addict with his pills
you held on with all your might.

But time had other plans for us
as it took your hand from mine
found us a different lover's lust
yet still, for each other we pine.

So, as the summer's days grew late
and winter put up a fight
we both resigned to cursing fate
whose timing wasn't right.

A BROKEN CUP

Why is my mug broken, says
a whimpering voice from within,
when the voice without says nothing
and hardly knows where it's been.

Who broke my little mug?
The one I'd used for tea,
the one I'd thought I'd gotten rid of
the day that you'd left me.

Tears stream down reddened cheeks
for this thing I'd long forgot
whilst these broken shards of porcelain
remind me I have not.

WILTED ROSE

you were the gardener and I your rose
all white in a field of red
you stopped to admire me
brought me inside
gave me all that you thought
i'd needed to survive
and the next morning
found me dead

YOUR HATE

You've made it your mission to hate me
in all that I am, for all that I do
and in some misguided way you place
the blame on me for hurting you.

But when will you learn that love alone hurts
that its battles are lost before they are done?
You see not that we both hurt each other
and neither you nor I our battles won.

THE SCARS YOU DO NOT SEE

there are more scars beneath my skin
than the ones you wish to count
as you list the features you admire
you choose to leave resilience out

I have worked hard for the scars you don't see
and worked harder still to hide them
but each one lives inside of me
though they may rise, settle, and rise again

a lesson learned, a wound unhealed
a breaking point reached but never broken
these are the splintered qualities of me
which you regard with little notice

fractured hearts from past lovers lost
waiting rivers of tears from somewhere within
lies that still haunt me, insults that still taunt me
choirs singing doubt to the bones beneath my skin

I will never be that idea of perfection
never rise from the pedestal you laid out for me
because of the scars beneath my skin
all the scars you do not see

THE QUEEN OF BROKEN HEARTS

There she goes, the Queen of Broken Hearts,
whose revels end in misfortune for all
and each sorry soul to cross her bloodied path
leaves its battered heart at the base of her bed.

There she goes, the Queen of Broken Hearts,
whose façade of innocence reels in all
the painted whore so branded and blamed
all men beware the devil that lies within.

There she goes, the Queen of Broken Hearts,
flaunting the image she created to trick
the likes of simple minds and shallow hearts who
dreamt only of perfection behind her weary eyes.

There she goes, the Queen of Broken Hearts,
whose tear-stained rosy-red cheeks mask only
the blue of her heart and the black of her soul
or so claim the men whose egos she has toppled.

There she goes, the Queen of Broken Hearts,
wearing the crown of rings too willingly given
to trap her, keep her, cage her in the loves
that loved only themselves and an idea that never was.

There she goes, the Queen of Broken Hearts,
no more woman than monster is she,
stalking the world for the next man to fall
and whose precious heart will be once broken too…

So branded be I, the Queen of Broken Hearts,
for once breaking hearts of the men who saw only
an idea of perfection and standards never met
and in true love though seeking never found…

Blame me, for I am the Queen of Broken Hearts,
but in all your painful angst willingly forget
that once broken was your shallow beating heart
a thousand times broken this weary heart of mine.

TOXIC

I feel the poisons crawling up
the spiderweb veins that line my wrists
spoiling all that I am and see
touching all with trembling fingertips.

I was never before this way
this foul green-eyed monster clings
with all his friends to me in wait
to spring on victims I have yet to meet.

The disease that festers in my brain
poisons my very heart and soul,
but I was never once this way
begging and breaking with all that I know.

Not 'til you showed me your love's drug
dosed me 'til I could breathe no more
to share in toxicity's enthrall
and left me pleading for another go.

But blame on you I shall not bequeath,
though it be your sheath I may recall,
for on this day I will admit
that it was I who let the toxic in.

THE DEATH OF ROMEO AND JULIET

We had it good, too good while it lasted,
our simple brief but sweet attraction
two souls bound tight so not even starlight
could find its home between your heart and mine.

We'd lace our hands and carry our dreams
in satchels stolen one midsummer's day
and leave two separate trails in favour
of the road we'd walk alone but together.

The stars kept our secrets, moonlight lined our beds
as she and all her sky-bound disciples played witness
to promises we thought we'd keep sacred
for more than a fortnight, but time had other plans.

We became the air the other needed to breathe,
the shifting ground beneath cautious feet,
the missing half to a broken whole that we
thought we could mend if we tried. We were wrong.

Soon, screams and tears accompanied us to bed,
and silence set our tables at each meal,
smiles were plastered on with stage makeup,
but our broken hearts still kept in time.

We found ourselves once more walking through
the tired paths of whose revels had long ended
dragging our feet with our hearts in battered tow
along the road together but more alone than ever.

And when the velvet curtain finally closed heavy
over poisoned corpses that we once owned, and yet
our degraded souls were cast away to other turmoils
as applause swelled for the death of Romeo and Juliet.

WERE IT JUST A SMILE

Years of not knowing have brought lines to his face
Years of just wishing have left longing in her eyes
The dreaming and wanting in this ballad blue
Could be forgotten, were it just a smile.

The echo of feeling in the shadow of laughs
That reaches out to bridge their hollow divide
Whose obvious lust each's character caress
Might be overlooked, were it just a smile.

And the shiver on skin and the grin undenied
The pulsing in chests that races to be heard
The blush on the cheeks forgotten to be covered
Wouldn't hurt so, were it just a smile.

But dawn forces recall of the passions long faded
That time has left simmering, waiting to boil
Where love may never grow but lies steady souls
Sharing all in that not just a smile.

WHERE LOVE CAN NEVER BE

Were I to speak of love to you
I would get lost in the chill of blue eyes
and bluer stories with happy endings
the likes of which occur only in dreams.

A story so intimate would force a curse
upon the very stars that bound it,
to which two souls and two paths shall ever cross
and whose confident strides, when meet will falter.

I could speak of the silent passion
that has grown in the gaps between divided worlds
and how action ponders in the wake of ever
a many chance encounter's false coincidence.

And how a lingering longing leaves behind
caged hearts of our own ironclad design
unbreaking, despite their bond and fear
what prospect and promise should yet possess.

So we may sit in silence over shared cups of tea,
contemplating politics and people, as fleeting
and fickle as the ever-changing weather
and avoid those gaps in conversations where
you should know, as well as I,
resides this love that can never be.

TORTUROUS TREACHEROUS HEART OF MINE

Torturous treacherous heart inside
to lust after that which walks ever further
and in blindness seeks out its own destruction
for a need it cannot dream to fill

To sit opposed that which resonates with
the deepest of enchantments and darker desires
wicked, though kind in intent may be
stills the beating to an almost break

For eyes that look upon such desire
that which life will not permit
yet, in glances shared by confidants
caress each second as though infinite

Torturous treacherous heart of mine
that beats to a tune it will never sing
though patient in its wait will stay
and of idyllic peace may only dream

WORLD'S STOP

Who gave you the power to stop
the world's revolving 'round the sun
like a jam in the revolving hotel doors
we used to ride in circles 'round
back when we were in love?

Who gave you the ring of keys
to lock the chest that holds my heart
and toss it deep below the waves
of the seas we once travelled carelessly
back when we were in love?

And who told you that you could leave
and walk away from all we'd done
and all we were, and all we'd known
and leave me writhing, crying alone
and wondering where I'd gone wrong?

...I did...
...I guess...
...I did so.

PERFECT BROKE THE CAMEL'S BACK

Our vows were strained by the stretches of time
we spent at other ends of other universes
trying to rekindle flames that we'd long since left
to simmer 'til they were not more than embers
in the hearth that once warmed our home.

But restraint and idealism dared not poke
at the flecks that glittered between the ash
fearing their soiling with soot and sorrow
and tainting the memories we kept in photographs
that sit on the shelves we allowed to gather dust.

It was then I realized loves fickle attraction
to the manicured ways of shallow hearts
and how these could never reach the endless depths
of who we were, and how our own longing
for perfection is what broke the camel's back.

NOVEMBER

we birds of a feather
who took flight whenever
as we said forever
and soared higher together
thought together was better
and said never say never
flying tangled and tethered
soon lost our endeavours
teased by other pretty feathers
and lost track of forever
thinking best wasn't better
and replaced never with whatever…
but I still remember
the late of November
we birds of warmer weather
never did weather that storm.

A LOVE THAT NEVER DIES

Here lies the still-beating heart
of a love that never dies
but whose casket has been sealed
by Death's spindly fingers
and tucked in by the dirt
on which it once walked free.

FRUIT AND NUT

In the year 1830, hazelnuts were introduced to the chocolate bar-making process by Charles-Amédée Kohler. This was the beginning of what history has come to known as *combination bars*. Nowadays, combination bars define the subgroup of chocolate confections which mix fruits, nuts, nougat, etc., adding a different dimension to the already delectable treat.

The following poems focus on the little things that we fall in love with that make life that much more pleasurable. These things tend to be the easiest to profess love for, as they speak to the truths about us, reflected in the external world. Cities, pets, friends, family, all are fair game when it comes to platonic love.

These poems, like their chocolatey counterpart, are fun, sweet, and in some cases, just a little nutty.

IN THE CITY THAT NEVER SLEEPS

Who knows what you'll find
in this city of lights and sounds and sights
at all hours of both day and night
this city, it never sleeps.

Music rings out on every street corner
clothing and food for our eyes to devour
bookshops that could've been castles await
in this city that never sleeps.

The hardworking folks catch the metro at 6
sitting next to the drunkards who have yet to return
from the wild Tuesday nights under neon lights
lining the city that never sleeps.

History comes to life before your eyes
strolling down the pathways of kings that were once
more than renewed cobblestone and patches of green
sprouting a city that never sleeps.

Museums of art and halls of science sit
quietly watching the pitter patter of city feet
along the busy bustling sidewalks and alleys
of the city whose patrons never sleep.

Coffee shops beckoning a young writer to stop
to plant herself firmly in the seat by the sill
a coffee in hand, a journal at her side
to detail the city that never sleeps.

And stories will be written of the sauntering songs
and all-consuming sights and scents
and the curious personas that flit about their days
in this city that never sleeps.

CITY OF GLASS

light and mystery leap from your corners
your people move with unrivalled vigor
through your winding alleyways
filled with wilder twisted tongues
as pastry scents saunter through baker's windows
and streetcars chime their scheduled stops
we stroll the street that queens once walked
for fish and chips and chardonnay
and cross to kings in parallel
for coffee on a chilly day
until we reach the greater lake
where into greyer skies reach hands
of glass and steel from a shimmering skyline
to the heavens above.

DOREEN

The stately matriarch returns to her vanity
applies rouge to the lips age has wrinkled, not ruined.
Her hair has grown frosty and her eyes too, cold,
but her beauty and mind glitter ever bright like
the rubies dangling from her all-hearing ears.

She fluffs her feather-white hair with pride
the same way she has for the past seventy years
and spritzes perfume in clouds 'round her neck
with dainty hands and elegantly glittered fingers
listening to Sinatra on the radio time left on her shelf.

This century is not like the last, she thinks
as she sweeps her draping pant leg from the floor,
remembering how only fifty years before,
though it feels to her like yesterday's trials,
those trousers of hers would've need be a dress.

She is woman, she is strength, toweringly statuesque
as she rises from the vanity, far from being vain,
steps out into the world that welcomes her only
as mother and grand, and no longer the jewel
that sent a thousand ships to sea.

Time glitters in her eyes as she watches
the youth of her line unravel the wrappings
of gifts her own hands worked hard to provide
wondering how another century will go by
and if her deathly date is finally dressed to leave.

CAROL

Ode to the grandmother who's always there
to give loving squeezes and twirl my hair.

To the woman who works hard for a living
who is kind and knows no bounds when giving.

Who feeds all the creatures that she finds astray
and helps all who cross her path on the way.

Whose one child surprised her by having three
and who loves each grand to an equal degree.

To the woman whose pancakes keep us fed
and who taught us all to keep level heads.

Whose pride in us shines through unfazed eyes,
who seeks out the beauty in simple skies.

No better example could I ever find
of a grandmother as wonderful as mine.

OLD FRIEND

Your laugh is comforting all on its own
your smiles are my remedy
a hug from you brings drought to storms
oh, how I cherish you, old friend.

From toddlers to teens, we've managed to grow
though twenties have gone we neglect our age
and time mark only our faces, not chats
that I share with you, old friend.

When our long hair begins to grey
and our brittle bones ache like our mothers before
stay at my side 'til death claims his bride
forever shall we two be friends.

LANGUAGE

Never by a language have I ever been enamoured
as by that which tantalizes the tongue
and as such would see speaking turn to song
where words become poems of their own accord
and tones the harpsichord melodically strummed
whereby subjecting one to love is listening
as foreign sounds emotions raise
spine tingling in nature as the culture ascends
to meet the romance of its words on page
and masters of the music make
melodies of most intimate intonation
these keepers of keys to linguistical gates
harmonious heaps our hearts so render
and to the naysayers I say once more
that if this ballad finds breath not taken
and understanding unspoken depths
cause only evasive apprehension—then
never by a language have you ever been enamoured
and sadly speak you only for to comprehend.

SISTER LOVE

We may fight, and kick, and scream
and say horrible things that we don't mean.

We may tease and pull at each other's hair
and make life with each other a living nightmare.

But here in our wilderness truth is found
we still keep each other safe and sound.

Sisters are not just blood but bond
we are harmony and melody, compliments of song.

PROTECTOR

Matter not your height or age
my protector, my brother sweet
you swing at those who hurt me, tease me
my rescuer in hours of need
the *off-limits caller*
the *he who's always there*
the *village idiot* in my times of despair
oh brother, my brother
whatever did I do
to deserve a protector
as loving as you.

MUSIC

when words fail
when chords feel
and lullabies speak louder than
love notes in scented envelopes
and getting lost is not frowned upon
where melodies bring back memories
and the heart hears more than the ears
and sounds bring smiles and tears
and stifle any hidden fears
that love is music
and music
is love

IN LOVE WITH LOVE ITSELF

Whoever would have said a thing
as falling in love with love itself
must have seen your charming grin
that you share with millions else.

He must have fallen for thousands of hands
holding rings and things of all valuable sorts,
and the whisperings of lust from varied lands
and their escapades with other cohorts.

He who once fell in love with love
must have known of its terrible charm
and longed for freedom's white feathered dove
when he spoke of the caged heart's harm.

Fallen was he for the picturesque
the Madonnas on the silver screen
who swoon to be courted and turn in jest
and marry the love of their dreams.

But in contemporary rests false romance's pearls
solidified by moving pictures on digital shelves
for the lovers of the technological world
fell madly in love with only love itself.

PRALINES

This final type of chocolate, also referred to as *truffles,* was created by Belgian Chocolatier Jean Neuhaus Junior in 1912. His development of the chocolate shell allowed for chocolates to be filled with soft fillings. Some of the more popular fillings are cream, caramel, and liquor-coated fruits, to name a few.

This delicate treat shows that it's not always what's on the outside that counts, especially as we curate our outsides to better hide our insides. These poems are all about loving what's on the inside and embracing ourselves, for every drop of caramel or liquor-coated cherry that fills our centre.

These poems are dedicated to self-love, and like their namesake, leave you with a soft and gooey feeling inside.

BE STEADY MY HEART

beat only when ready
when the idea of love
is no longer imagination
and feels more real
than breathing

LEAVING

Blessed was the day I left
the lovers whose hands built only
greenhouses to cage me
in favour of those who admired
the chaos of my jungle
and whose footprints grew
flowers in their wake.

SETTLE NO MORE

no more will I settle
for being less than myself
for fitting into molds
made by other people
for people other than me

only I will decide if and when
to shave my rougher edges
so that our pieces might fit
to curb my many tangents
so our lines might eventually meet

and if my wood needs work
I will decide when to fix it
and if my glass is cracked
only I will choose the repair
unbound by the ideas of who I should be…

tethered only to the longing in my heart
I will settle no more.

THE MARKS OF BEING ME

Many a battle have I fought
to wear the crown I now brandish
like the swords they used to hurt me
but only made me stronger
made me fierce, made me hungry
like the lioness that prowls the pride lands
I shall no longer be brought down
by the hyenas who laugh at me
at scars they'll never comprehend
and dance in circles with their cackles
hoping to bring me low, make me tremble
but no longer will I falter, I will not break
for I am the guardian of my sanity
keeper of scars, warden of the traumas
they wished would define me
—and almost did, before I grew
like a phoenix from the remains
of the ashen shell it used to haunt,
like the rose on its stem of thorns
that dares only the brave to touch it,
I am growth, I am rebirth
I am a work in progress
I am the unfinished works of a mad young writer
learning to love the scars I keep
and the marks of being me.

TO LOVE THYSELF

a gift it is to love thyself
a love unlike any other
for only you can know which are
the points that you find tender
and the things that bring you pleasure
to be loved and loved forever
unbound from the fleeting whims of life
or time and space's choking grip
and other lovers' tethers
whereby you and you alone may share
in true love's blissful forevers
alone, just you and you together.

BEING AND TO BE

to walk away from all
—the things i thought might but never served me
—the ideas that must have once defined me
—the jobs whose titles were once important
—the people whose approval i once needed
seemed like a daunting task
once, before I decided
to give up on this *being me*
and learned who *me* truly was
and how to simply *be*.

CHOCOLATES OF MY OWN LIKING

When I was young, I ate milk chocolate bars,
the kinds the kids brought to school,
whatever the wrapper was fine by me.
And though I enjoyed the sugary treats,
I found I liked more their company.

So I grew up a bit and ate white chocolate bars,
because that was what the avant garde did,
and suddenly my playtime became chitchat
with others who knew lots about decidedly little
and whose gossip filled my ears, but not my stomach.

I grew up some more and ate fruit and nut bars
because they were nutty like I thought I should be,
but being nutty became being lonely
(at least I remember that's what they all told me)
and being nutty and lonely was not to be.

In between I somehow learned to avoid
the chocolates that brought me decadent peace
the darkest of chocolates which made me most happy
understanding wrongly I should learn to fit in
when what I didn't understand rightly was me.

Now I have seen through the fads and the flings
and the many things that other people do
to make them blend in and feel that they fit
like making sure to eat the same exact chocolate
whilst me and my dark chocolate stay far from view.

I CHOSE ME

When we met and fell in love
we fell like shooting stars
decided in the fate we saw
but whose trajectories led away.

You fell for the idea of me
and I in silence fell for the love
I felt because you showed it
to the girl you wished I was.

Then you asked for forever vows
for me to run away with you
and have three kids and a house on a hill
and do the things your parents do.

But I was never raised that way
the love you want was never me
but what you thought that I should do
and who you wanted me to be.

I know another will fill your bed
and hold your hand at the altar's steps
have the family with the white-picket fence
and walk with you to Heaven's gates.

But I couldn't be that girl for you
without losing the person I wanted to be
so it broke my heart to let you go
but I knew it was time that I chose me.

I WILL TAKE MY TIME

I hear the ticking of the clock
at the other end of the desk
the one that counts the seconds by
waiting for me to grow up and grow old,
and be all the things I detest.

My father set its clicking gears
my mother painted its face
my mentors taught me to read the thing
my job taught me to need the thing
but it's grown into something I hate.

I wondered what would happen to me
if I chucked it out the room
Would I still feel a pressure inside?
Would I still know which path to take?
Would I still do all the things—I'll admit
—I never wanted to?

I turned to face the world outside
where my eyes hitch on a tree,
the one that grew on its own time
in its own place, with its own mind
and turned into what it was meant to be.

So I picked up the ticking tocking clock
and hurled it far from me,
let time fly by somewhere else—for someone else,
but I will take my time in life
and grow into the person I decide to be.

THE GIRL IN THE MIRROR

The girl in the mirror staring back at me
once mocked the very way I stood
cringed at the gap between my teeth
laughed at the frizz in my hair.

The girl in the mirror once wished on stars
hoping to look more like the models in magazines
than the waitress at the bar beneath the house
that no one ever called pretty.

This girl was shunned and shook off
and slowly resigned to the lacklustre life
she thought she'd somehow earned on account
of her exceptional ordinariness.

But the girl in the mirror looks no more
at the way her hips don't curve out
or the wildly stray hairs to be plucked
from the edges of her brow to follow fashion.

The girl in the mirror sees now only stars
in the reflection her own eyes make.
She sees fire and power and working long hours
to become much more than just a pretty face.

This girl in the mirror mocks no more
nor does she relent to the words others say
in their meager attempt to satisfy themselves
as their egos and insecurities keep them enslaved.

SELF-RESPECT

Self-respect is not given
to those too lighthearted
to see their own worth or merit
and thus ask upon others
to grant them their freedom
from the biased ideologies
and broken rhetoric
that has convinced us all
—we must obey.

Self-respect is only earned
once the wearer becomes the wielder
of the shame that long latched them
with doubt and dangerous disregard
to locks of *pretense* and *purpose*
whose keys dangle heavily
around unwitting necks
ready to set their wearer free
—waiting only to be unclasped.

THESE ARE THE CHAINS

These are the chains that once were cast
to keep my wanton spirit beholden
locked up by societal wantings
and wishes of those whose shoes I wore not
and whose many names I did not own.

I wore these chains with derelict pride
wishing to be seen as the queen of pack mules
for I was good but could be better
and never in questioning mind did ask
to whose broken post my soul was tethered.

Adorned me once, but now no longer
these chains of doubt and duties told
broken only by defiance of that
which radiated with a courage earned
and a mind no longer captive.

IN THE END

In the end, my dear
it shall only be You and I
a battle You've fought fiercely
to keep at bay, to keep away
and keep Your other soldiers in tow
but still, my dear
in life there is nothing
that will not be not stripped
as bare as the babe is born from the womb
time will take all from You
and all the trivialities
to which You wish to cling
will mean nothing when it's just us two
and so, my dear
satisfy Yourself as yet
Your tomorrows are still Your own
and the youth may ponder fondly
and fawn over You at night
for in the end, in truth my dear,
coddle now Your longing's fear,
it shall only be You and I.

OTHER WORKS IN THIS COLLECTION...

If you enjoyed this book, please feel free to leave a review of it on your favourite sites. These reviews help small-time authors like me reach new audiences and are much appreciated!

Stay up to date on L. M. Sanguinette's new releases and giveaways by signing up for her mailing list or following her on social media. Find all the links at the page below:

https://linktr.ee/lmsanguinette/

Be on the lookout for more books coming soon!

ABOUT THE AUTHOR

L. M. Sanguinette was born on a small island in the Caribbean, where the palm trees watched over her like giants and the sea crept up to her feet to say hello. Ever since she was little, she surrounded herself with tales of fantasy and magic, hoping that one day, she too would be involved in a story like the ones that captured her imagination.

Years—and many rewatching's of Avatar the Last Airbender—later, she is happily living in the worlds that her mind created, filling her bookshelves with more books than she will ever read, and practising her own version of magic.

When she's not sitting at the computer, she can be found snorkelling near forgotten shores, twisting from silks that hang from the ceilings, or in one of the many hidden coffee shops of Madrid, conversing with the spirits of the old city and dreaming up new adventures.

OTHER WORKS

Welcome to Visanthe (#1, Legend of the Stones)
Visanthe in Ruin (#2, Legend of the Stones)
Visanthe Rising (#3, Legend of the Stones)

Of Arrows and Roses

The Days I Dream of Coffee
The Days I Dream of Chocolate
The Days I Dream of Chardonnay